Examining Post 2008 You[th] in the United Kingdom, C[o] the Disengaged and Disenfranchised Consensus?

Table of contents

Table of contents 1

Abstract 2

Introduction 3

Chapter One – Non-Conventional Political Participation 9

Chapter Two - Examining and Improving Conventional Participation and Associated Issues 30

Chapter Three – Conclusions 46

Bibliography 49

Examining post 2008 youth political participation in the United Kingdom, confirming or questioning the disengaged and disenfranchised consensus?

Abstract

This study contains a thorough examination of youths in the political stage since the post 2008 era. By doing so , it looks to answer the question of whether young people are engaged politically. By looking at the methods available to them and the associated extent of engagement ,it is possible to determine the degree of political engagement shown and wheatear this constitutes political engagement , developing a correlation, inverse or not , in terms of young people's political engagement since 2008. This will be done by assessing the events of the post 2008 era in which young people have been directly involved and academia produced in this time. Assessing both conventional forms of engagement in the form of electoral

3 Examining post 2008 youth political participation in the United Kingdom, confirming or questioning the disengaged and disenfranchised consensus?

participation and non-conventional forms such as protest and E-petitions, the study broadly supports there has been no substantial change to youth political engagement, with mixed results throughout the period across conventional and non-conventional participation. Finding neither form appears to be associated with nor have had any radical changes, but that contemporary political participation has evolved. Young people are increasingly exploring all avenues given to participate politically. This study determines young people between the ages of 16-25 as this age range is most capable of being able to participate whilst still being defined as young people. Political participation is any method utilised to exert political influence. Political engagement can range from voting and protesting to vandalism and acts of terrorism and civil disobedience (European union, "Glossary on youth").

Introduction

Context and hypothesis

This study aims to examine whether young people are politically engaged within the UK since the year 2008. The post 2008 era has been diverse in terms of political engagement and the methods used to participate, questioning the idea of disenfranchisement and disengagement amongst young people. Often this is based on electoral engagement and no other forms hence this essay has a wide scope. The context behind this study is a number of contemporary media sources suggesting young people are disengaged and disenfranchised, being politically engaged (Henn &

Examining post 2008 youth political participation in the United Kingdom, confirming or questioning the disengaged and disenfranchised consensus?

Oldfield, 2016), ("Most young lack interest in politics - official survey", 2014) as well as wider academic concern of the same .This concern demonstrate both the contextual relevancies and importance of the subject. The study expects to find that young people are engaged increasingly through un-conventional means and not through conventional processes and consequently are still politically engaged but are stereotyped due to a lack of electoral participation. This essay defines the key terms of young people as being between the ages 16 and 25 as this is the age of most people who are capable of participation whilst still classed as young adults whilst participation is defined as any method by which political influence is exerted but must meet Akram's (2009) requirements of being planned and considered.

Ethics and ethical statement

Ethical risks need examining as this project relates to individuals, their political activities and choices, specifically the preference to engage politically . This project examinees individuals written works through academic submissions and articles alongside data from individuals given in the form of surveys and polling data. All information and its analysis are essential for this project. Only relevant or required data will be utilised to minimise ethical implications.

This project contains minimal ethical risks , having no primary data collection or analysis, however ethical risk remains when examining academic doctrines and theories, such as academic's skewing research based upon personal bias or conducting un-ethical research. To counteract ethical implications, academic doctrines or articles will be appraised to scrutinise for bias and discarded if uncovered. Academic articles and theories have ethical risks if based on surveys, however these will have been regulated and done in a way to minimise ethical risks. Surveys and polling data are anonymised except for essential data, minimising the ethical implications, and being carried out by regulated organisations who follow strict procedures to minimise ethical risks, therefore ethical implications are negated for analysis of these data sources. News articles and supporting contextual sources are only used if reliable and suitably academic and relevant , and likewise have minimal ethical risks.

Method

The method employed examines current academic findings , polling and survey data and key events to examine youth political participation and assessing the extent to which this can be seen to have constituted political engagement from young people. Employing this method allowed a focus on the youth demographic and allowed a wider scope of examination in terms of forms of engagement.

Literature review

Youth political participation is a pertinent issue in contemporary society, not purely in the United Kingdom but across established western

Examining post 2008 youth political participation in the United Kingdom, confirming or questioning the disengaged and disenfranchised consensus?

democracies and further afield (Clark, 2018). Disengagement can be seen as transnational. Survey data demonstrates 37% of European 15–25 year olds express a political interest (Ogris & Westphal, 2005) (Farthing, 2010) a worrying minority. Academics contend young people aren't engaged politically. Putnam (1995) suggests this in America, whilst Furlong & Cartmel (2007) study this across the global north with similar findings. Ekman & Amnå (2012) contest that populations are becoming more disengaged from traditional methods of political engagement , a broad academic consensus supported by Dalton (2008) and Grönlund & Milner (2006), with some specifying young people are the most disengaged (Patterson, 2002) (Teixeira, 1992) (Carpini, 2000) (Kaid, Mckinney, & Tedesco, 2007) (Karbach & Pleyers, 2014) and (Keeter, Zukin, Andolina, & Jenkins, 2002). Studies substantiate that significant forms of participation are declining amongst the youth demographic (Deželan & Lisney, 2015). This consensus comes from across the global spectrum of long-established democracies and supports the theory that this is a serious and transnational issue. The idea of exclusion from politics is consistent across academic papers (Manning, 2010). The decline in electoral participation is argued to be an obvious symptom of broader lack of engagement (Longo & Meyer, 2006).

However other academics propose that engagement , especially in relation to youth, is not declining but diversifying, and that what constitutes participation has become broader and more encompassing.

7   Examining post 2008 youth political participation in the United Kingdom, confirming or questioning the disengaged and disenfranchised consensus?

Van Deth (2001) argues that research has previously focused solely on conventional participation. Norris (2003), Zukin, Keeter, andAndolina (2006) and Sloam (2007) both contest that the use of social media and the internet has changed political participation and led to increases in unconventional forms. Henn & Foard (2011) argue conventional processes are the problem and this causes the disengaged perception. Stolle, Hooghe, & Micheletti (2005) supports this suggesting informal methods are favoured by young people. Forbrig (2005) alludes expansion of politics has been synonymous with expanded definitions of participation and increasing options to impact politics. Similarly Marsh (2016) suggests new methods young people see as more pertinent to their demographic are becoming prevalent. This demonstrates debate surrounding contemporary political participation as a fall in conventional participation could be indicative of a wider decline in participation. Although, a fall in conventional participation may be counteracted by an increase in unconventional forms of participation, something this study aims to assess.

Democratic theories

Many democratic theories verify the problem of participation in democracies, most notably these imply democracy decays should citizens fail to participate. The levels of participation are important as it directly impacts the extent representation of the legislatures (Rosenstone & Hansen, 2009). Highton (2009) states that scholars are occupied with outcomes not objectives. Bendix & Huntington (1971) contend that

Examining post 2008 youth political participation in the United Kingdom, confirming or questioning the disengaged and disenfranchised consensus?

modern societies are defined by higher levels of participation. Sloam (2011) presents the idea that generational replacement causes political changes and that generations participation influences politics. Distrust is often perpetuated as a motivation for lack of participation (Almond & Verba, 1963), but other factors can be seen in literature. Rosenstone & Hansen (2003) dispute the influence of distrust in political participation. Blais (2000) suggests citizens only participate as a result of their civic duty.

Definitions

Academics use varying definitions in relation to youth political participation. Political participation and youth both have no set definitions in academic terms. Ekman & Amnå (2012) argue that the use of definitions constitutes "conceptual stretching". The varying academic definitions make them ineffective but contemporary definitions are encompassing. Berger (2009) defines engagement as all-encompassing, ranging from donating money to political rallies. Brady, Verba, & Schlozman (1995) define participation as occasions for influencing governments and their apparatus. Likewise ,Conway (2000) defines it as such but includes influencing political decisions. Smith, Lister, Middleton, & Cox (2005) states that contemporary participation necessitates a wide-ranging definition to include all forms of participation something which although not widely supported is notable.

Scrutiny of literature

9   Examining post 2008 youth political participation in the United Kingdom, confirming or questioning the disengaged and disenfranchised consensus?

Many studies view engagement purely as electoral participation, (Brady, Schlozman, & Verba, 1999) especially before the new millennium (Finch, Verba, & Nie, 1974). Contemporary definitions are broader (Ekman & Amnå, 2012) limiting the usefulness of older studies but not discrediting them but meaning they should be taken cautiously. (Grönlund & Milner, 2006) argue knowledge of the system and individuals is a pre-requisite for democracies to operate effectively. Many studies lack the wide-ranging definitions necessary to capture the most prominent forms of participation. Furthermore, much of the literature is dated and evolving methods mean this presents issues.

Chapter One – Non-Conventional Political Participation

Historical context

Historically citizens or factions have employed non-conventional forms of political participation, ostensibly through rebellions, terrorist attacks and protests encompassing political elements as contributing factors. These occasions demonstrate non-conventional participation has wide-ranging rationales. Examining historical occurrences establishes the context and causations of occurrences of non-conventional participation. This is imperative to comprehend, as it pertains relevance to contemporary non-conventional participation, furthermore, ascertaining that non-conventional participation is not merely a contemporary phenomenon.

Examining post 2008 youth political participation in the United Kingdom, confirming or questioning the disengaged and disenfranchised consensus?

The Roman Republic underwent a notable occurrence of non-conventional participation with the Third Servile War; an insurgency led by absconded slaves including infamously Spartacus; congregating 120,000 followers and surmounting security apparatus (Peterson, 2013). Following deliberation, the senate dispatched eight legions, headed by several proficient generals, to disperse this menace. (Appian , "The Histories of Appian ,THE CIVIL WARS Book I").

Conceivably the impetus behind the dissidence was an undertaking by the slave class to ameliorate themselves through banditry and looting. Nevertheless, it is contended the underlying motivation was halting the prevalent maltreatment of slaves. Legal statute specified slaves were not people but assets. By definition proprietors could victimise slaves without repercussions under the legal framework (Shumway, 1901). The preponderance of the class was enlisted in arduous physical labour. With inconsequential legal protection it is obvious therefore they sought transformation, understanding there existed minimal likelihood of this unless exploiting non-conventional participation in an endeavour to alter circumstances. Demonstrating the motivation behind the insurgency was the privation of conventional participation accordingly, turning to non-conventional approaches, incorporating insurrection to achieve this. Even though the objectives remain indefinite, but they certainly encompassed terminating servitude or ameliorating treatment for persons in servitude, the insurrection was fruitless. This demonstrates an early form of non-conventional participation.

Terrorism has also constituted non-conventional participation, often triggered by a scarcity of recourse to partake in conventional participation or a deficiency of attainments through these organs. The Irish Republican Army (IRA), a political and terrorist organisation espoused attaining home rule and later the unification of Ireland, employed non-conventional participation in an endeavour to attain their objectives. Irish sectarianism has been a byzantine issue , enduring so. As well as terrorist activities, political proceedings were undertaken. Terrorism was ultimately political as established by their aims, themselves intensely political. Scholars contemplate whether the application of terrorism gave the IRA moderate success as terrorism perpetrated by them coerced and necessitated the British state to negotiate with them. The Council for Foreign Relations asserts "[a] stalemate convinced the IRA's political wing, Sinn Fein, to open secret talks with the British government" (Moran, 2006), demonstrating terrorism was not wholly efficacious in attaining the objectives, but nonetheless guaranteed the IRA was perceived as a credible threat by the British state. Although conventional participation was utilised, this alone was not effective, demanding non-conventional participation to fulfil the objectives. The IRA was partially successful in using non-conventional participation, However not harnessing political processes alongside would have been unavailing.

Examining post 2008 youth political participation in the United Kingdom, confirming or questioning the disengaged and disenfranchised consensus?

A pre-eminent accomplishment of non-conventional participation was the American Civil Rights Movement which questioned the discrimination of minorities prevalent within American Society. Compared with other historical cases, the American Civil Rights Movement accomplished nearly wholesale attainment, predominantly without resorting to violence. Prominent milestones encompassed the Birmingham bus boycott, the passing of the Civil Rights Act 1964 and Voting Rights Act 1995, ensuring federal aegis of the 14th and 15th constitutional amendments, hitherto although unconstitutional, minorities had been discriminated against. Incapable of using conventional participation due to the entrenched nature of segregation and discrimination, the movement used non-conventional participation such as boycotts, protest marches, strikes and sit-ins. Although discrimination in America remains, it is now minuscule in comparison .

Importance of non-conventional forms of participation and examples

Non-conventional participation takes varying compositions, ranging from illegal to minor peaceful activities to attain political ambitions. As the historical context demonstrates, non-conventional participation has brought about significant results and changes. Non-conventional political participation is defined as any political activity not included in the realms of traditional democratic process; including illegal, immoral or unusual forms of engagement. In the contemporary climate this may include signing online petitions or strike action and protests. Despite not directly impacting democratic processes and legislatures, non-conventional participation remains important, often being the articulation of those who endure disenfranchisement and disengagement with customary democratic systems. Non-conventional methods can be highly efficient at garnering fourth and third estate engagement ,for example it can be quicker to stage a protest than to lobby for legislative changes surrounding public policy. (Sigel, Barnes, & Kaase, 1980) set out unconventional forms of participation including political violence, strikes, boycotts, petitions and mass demonstrations; a range which may have evolved in the 21st century nonetheless giving contextualisation.

Democratic processes perpetually occur within set time frameworks since the 2011 Fixed-Term Parliaments Act (Blick, 2015) (Smith, Spain, & Glancey, 2015) , which ensures elections occur quinquennially unless several conditions are met. The Act was designed to effectuate the election cycle increasing stability and preventing governments calling elections when most beneficial for them. Although this ensured long periods between elections this may have caused many who feel disenfranchised to pursue non-conventional participation. Acts of non-conventional participation may be significant or imperative to the electorate. Alternatively, non-conventional participation may be a result of a government's breaking manifesto commitments or initiating policies the electorate disagrees with. The aforementioned reasons demonstrate

Examining post 2008 youth political participation in the United Kingdom, confirming or questioning the disengaged and disenfranchised consensus?

the importance of non-conventional participation, which is further evidenced by the historical context supporting some of the concepts suggested and demonstrates it is not merely a contemporary phenomenon. Although the historical cases do not relate to the youth age group, nor the time frame being examined, it remains pertinent.

Since 2008 many occasions have evidenced the importance of non-conventional participation within the 16 to 25 age demographic, varying from the tuition fees protests to forms of participation which are considered normative such as signing of e-petitions . These methods of non-conventional participation had significant impact upon life within the United Kingdom in the time scale this essay scrutinizes. Notably many of forms of engagement are more likely to involve young people as the issues at stake directly affect them, or due to a higher online presence, marking themselves as important political actors (Abrahams & Brooks, 2018) in comparison to the wider population; nonetheless there remain stereotypes to the types of engagement young persons are likely to conduct and their levels of political participation.

Illegal participation is often overlooked, being outside societal norms and contravening legal precedents, but may be contended to be a primary form of participation for those who are disenfranchised and disengaged with the conventional system The consensus is often that the most disenfranchised and disengaged demographic examined by this essay examines, could be more likely to use illegal participation. This should not necessarily mean that this participation is invalid, nor should it be disregarded, as this participation may be some of the most poignant and serious in terms of repercussions. The stereotypical terrorist is disengaged and disenfranchised. Terrorism, has a platitude of definitions. This essay uses the definition given by the prosecution body, the Crown Prosecution Service, "[terrorism is] the use or threat of action, ... designed to influence any ... government organisation or ... the public. ... for the purpose of advancing a political, religious, racial or ideological cause" ("Crown Prosecution Service - Terrorism", 2020). Terrorism is a political action even when not politically motivated; since the objectives have political repercussions . As such, membership of terrorist organisations is a political act although it may not be purely political often being a consequence of multiple socio-economic factors. Terrorism and membership of terror organisations is always a political action even if a by-product of other causes.

Home Office data, (Flatley, 2019) establishes a number of young people were arrested for terrorism offences, between 2001 and 2016. 52% of all persons arrested were under 30; equating to 1625 persons. 125 persons were under 18. Although askew from the time frame and age demographic examined, it indicates that those under 30 are more likely to be involved in terrorist activity. Therefore, if viewed as political engagement, this would demonstrate that under 30s are engaged but,

Examining post 2008 youth political participation in the United Kingdom, confirming or questioning the disengaged and disenfranchised consensus?

due to the multiple causes of radicalisation and inconsequential evidence, this is not a credible demonstration of non-conventional political engagement (Kirk-Wade & Allen, 2020). Examining prohibited organisations such as the BNP, which is political in aims and means, there are several studies which examine demographic which prevalently support the BNP. The 2010 EHRC report (Boon, 2010) studied those from age 18 + finding that males age 25 to 34 were more likely to support the BNP than other demographics although the difference was negligible. Another study suggests there is no age demographic prevalent in supporting the BNP (Biggs & Knauss, 2011). These studies demonstrate support for prohibited organisations is not an act of political participation which the 16-25 demographic make use of over other age demographics substantiating the theory that terrorism remains an outlet for only a minority across the general population and political spectrum. Furthermore, it is unlikely that individuals are doing so as an act of political participation, with little evidence to support terrorism as an act of political participation, but largely a result of socio-economic factors. A report into terrorist exploitation of youth alludes commonplace factors are: "searching for a group, ideologies, perceived or actual exclusion or physical threat, economic benefits [or] stability ..., and the idea of ... fame or respect and increasing personal connections. "(Darden, 2019). Virtually none of these relate to public policy or are political, purporting that supporting terrorism and prohibited groups is not likely nor significant as an act of engagement despite the historical context. Judging these

17   Examining post 2008 youth political participation in the United Kingdom, confirming or questioning the disengaged and disenfranchised consensus?

factors, terrorist actions are rarely considered or organised in the political sense per se, but are in terms of maximising public fear and disruption to communities. Despite political intentions, the actions themselves are non-political, therefore it is viable that terrorism does not satisfy Akram's requirement for political participation (Akram, 2009 in Furlong, 2014) despite being organised and considered. It is not inconceivable that in the future it may become an act of the politically disengaged and disenfranchised thus demonstrating the importance investigating this form of non-conventional engagement. Going forward it may be necessary to examine it in order to prevent terrorist actions such as those seen in the historical context, by looking at the political causes although these are few and far between.

The 2011 UK riots might be judged non-conventional participation. The average individual implicated was under 25 (Berman, 2014). Inequality, police brutality (Biggs, 2015), racism, gang culture and cuts (Platts-Fowler, 2016) are mooted as causes for the riots together notwithstanding the trigger was the police shooting of Mark Duggan (Bridges, 2012). Subsequent discussion indicated the Government's austerity policy was a primary factor (Kelsey, Mueller, Whittle, & Khosravinik, 2015). These factors demonstrate the events as political engagement yet so do the repercussions. Rioting yielded over £200 million of damage and costs to insurers and the taxpayer which included the looting of 2500 shops (Barentsen, 2013) (Treadwell, Briggs, Winlow, & Hall, 2012) (Greenwood,

2011), (Neligan, 2011) conceivably indicating rioting was an after effect of jaded youth partaking in delinquency and brutality (Clarke, 2011). Akram contends rioters are "marginalised subjects" whose actions result from the post-political climate (Akram, 2014). Berman notes 78% of individuals prosecuted afterwards appeared upon the National Benefit's database, increasingly likely to have free school meals and lower education and employment opportunities, typically denominating deprivation (Berman, 2011) (Flint & Powell, 2012). Rioting owing to impecuniousness, societal marginalisation and institutional inequality and racism is supported by academics (Keith, 1993) ,(Moran & Waddington, 2016) thus, supporting Akram's contention that the riots are "political protest against structural inequality", furthermore the catalyst begetting the insurrection is recognisably political (Treadwell, 2012). The then deputy prime minister stated the economic agenda pursed by the government would lead to violent unarrest (Younge, 2011).Together this supports arguments that the causes behind the riots were political and therefore were exploits of non-conventional political engagement.

Alternative theories propose rioting was a result of bored youths (Jahoda, 1982). Clarke also suggests this (Clarke, 2011) or was a form of community interaction (Gilroy, 2002), a representation supported by the government report which did not suggest political motivations (Department for Communities and Local Government , 2013). Akram suggests that political actions are considered and organised, (Akram 2009) underpinning assertions which suggest rioting was not politically motivated. Nonetheless much of the rioting was organised - both Twitter and BlackBerry Messenger were condemned for playing vital roles, allowing communication and organisation of rioters (Lewis, Adegoke, & Burch, 2012). Furthermore, it remains difficult to dissect the motivations behind individual rioters perhaps using political excuses for insurrection. The trigger cause was certainly political, and many other causes debated by academics, specifically austerity, have political elements. This demonstrates the factors were political, therefore the riots themselves were a form of political engagement as the objectives and causes were political., Even if there were more urgent and short-term factors, the long-term and structural causes were certainly political or politically caused.

The 2010 student protests attest to young people using non-conventional participation and it almost wholly represents the age demographic this essay pertains to. This was a response to the coalition government's threefold hiking of tuition fees; something the Liberal Democrat Party had pledged not to do (Hensby, 2017) ,demonstrating that politicians were undependable ,often a rationale for young people not conventionally participating (Bertsou, 2019) The protests were systematised by the National Union of Students and are political as antecedents of public policy decisions and purported to achieve renunciation of these (Kumar,

2011). The actions were marshalled and reasoned implying they are political (Akram, 2009) substantiating that conventional forms of participation failed, and accordingly young people deviated to non-conventional participation to attain their pretensions an idea supported by Reichert (Reichert, 2016). The protests were ineffectual, failing to garner a reversal in policy but triumphant in holding the Liberal Democrat Party to account, bringing about an apology from the former deputy Prime Minister Nick Clegg (Hillman, 2016) ("Students have not forgiven the Liberal Democrats for raising tuition fees", 2017). It is controverted they resulted in impairing electoral performance for the Liberal Democrats at forthcoming elections as it brought public attention to the inefficacity of the party to protect a core voter demographic (Cutts & Russell, 2015).

Academics have purported other causes were prevalent motivations for these protests (Mampaey, Wit, & Broucker, 2019), certifiable for a minority of participants but not in terms of the broader juggernaut, having unequivocal objectives and intentions which were predominantly peaceful denoting the arguments appertained in relation to the 2011 riots cannot be applied, principally tuition fee protests were ostensibly political in their disposition. Although fruitless, protesters assayed to revert a significant government policy, therefore it is generally accepted this was political engagement by young people primarily as it impacted those

21   Examining post 2008 youth political participation in the United Kingdom, confirming or questioning the disengaged and disenfranchised consensus?

under the age of 25 who were university students at the time or who may become so in the future.

Strikes demonstrate further youth non-conventional engagement, unlikely to be considered owing to the stereotypical mise-en-scène contiguous with strikes alongside expansive de-unionisation within the UK. Contemporary history authenticates multitudinous strikes involved young people. These include strikes at McDonald's restaurants and the school climate strikes. These strikes also demonstrate that young people have used non-conventional means in order to achieve political objectives. Akram states political actions must be planned and organised (Akram , 2009). This is gratified in both these occurrences however this composition will only review the 2019 McDonald's strikes due to the lack of reliable resources appertaining to the climate strikes. The McDonald's strikes were carried out to procure enhanced remuneration and ameliorate working conditions, political terms per se; the foremost McDonald's strikes in the UK occurred in 2017 at two separate locations ; Cambridge and Crayford (Kollewe & Slawson, 2017) over rudimentary remuneration and contractual conditions, supported by the then, leader of the Opposition and Labour Leader, Jeremy Corbyn, and other senior party figures and several trade unions. In the context of extensive political dissensus attaining to employment conditions and a number of protesters marching to Downing Street, these actions evidence this to be of political ramification (Murugesu, 2017) , (Chapman, 2019). Systematisation by trade unions denotes this action was organised and considered satisfying Akram's requisites for political participation (Akram, 2009). McDonald's UK state that the median age of their 120,000 employees is 20 years old, substantiating that this issue is pertinent to the age demographic this essay purports to, (Gould, 2010) , ("FAQS: McDonald's UK", no date). The restaurant sector chiefly employs a young workforce, possessing 3.2% trade union enrolment therefore employees are more likely to terminate the worker-employer relationship than to raise grievances (Owen, et al., 2019). Given this climate, strikes could be considered unlikely as political participation, additionally the context substantiates the wider sector rather than a sole transnational corporation is likely to impact young people's employment, remuneration and conditions.

The strike movement was colloquially known as "#mcstrike" and evoked by the American "fightfor$15" (Cant & Woodcock, 2020). The 2017 strike was abetted by left-wing organisation momentum and despite a lack of worker participation, managed to engender sizable media preoccupation, (Wood, 2020). Due to the 2017 strike, McDonalds improved renumeration at directly run sites and endorsed that franchisees did likewise. (Chapman, 2018). 2018 saw additional strikes take place in conjunction with other food sector workers from Weatherspoon's, McDonald's, TGI Fridays and Uber Eats (Cant & Woodcock, 2020). To some extent these actions were successful. Despite predominately failing to attain, a primary objective-, union recognition, the strikes obtained multiple minor and specific concessions centring around salaries, rotas and conditions. Weatherspoon's brought forward an increase in remuneration, abolished lower wage rates and added a night shift premium. Uber Eats allegedly increased its "boost" mechanism for deliveries, remunerating drivers thus resulting in an hourly wage increase (Cant & Woodcock, 2020). These campaigns were executed through a hybridisation of traditional union systematisation alongside social media campaigning; authenticating that unions were targeting the youth age demographic to participate. (Nowak & Hodder, 2019). The partaking unions and employees' objectives were political and can be comprehended as such, owing to political involvement of the unions, opposition politicians and the aim of achieving shifts in public policy and pay and conditions. Jones argues that the increase of youth conventional participation and consequently unconventional participation was synchronous and affiliated (Jones, 2018) alluding that the strike movement is contemporaneous with an expansive augmentation in youth political engagement. This strike is set against a backdrop of ostensible regression in union participation, however dissecting union participation insinuates a diminutive expansion in recent years. In 2018, 1 in 10 of the 16-19 demographic were union constituents, being a 1.2% increase on the previous year. The under 24 demographic similarly had an increase of 0.6%. Notwithstanding this, these years bucked the trend, with a decline over the previous decade in union affiliation, not just in the youth demographics but more comprehensively across the board. Conceivably in the contemporary socio-economic climate young people are re-

Examining post 2008 youth political participation in the United Kingdom, confirming or questioning the disengaged and disenfranchised consensus?

unionising in order to attain political aspirations and utilise collective bargaining together with other protections unionisation offers. ("Youth membership of unions grows amidst decades of decline", 2020). This is unconventional engagement due to the political complexion of the objectives as well as the wider societal and political policy implications surrounding strikes and union membership. There is also evidence linking union participation and conventional participation (McElwee, 2015). Barrett and Bruton-Smith suggest strike action and union membership is a collective extra-parliamentary form of political participation (Barrett & Brunton-Smith, 2017), remaining as such, especially in the age demographic examined by this essay, perhaps more so given the recent upturn in union membership.

Electronic petitions (E-petitions) have become increasingly employed since 2008; being a moderately contemporary advancement in the sphere of political engagement owing to the advent of the internet. 99% of individuals in the 16-44 age demographic in 2018 (the latest year for which figures were obtainable) are internet literate citizens corroborating the age demographic this essay appertains to are almost wholly internet proficient (Prescott, 2019), therefore being increasingly probable to use E-petitions, contrary to other demographics with inferior internet literacy. The two foremost websites in the UK are Gov.uk Petitions, which is government facilitated and carries issues before the legislature notwithstanding only permitting affairs which the UK legislature

25   Examining post 2008 youth political participation in the United Kingdom, confirming or questioning the disengaged and disenfranchised consensus?

superintends, and Change.org, a website allowing online petitions to be curated and handed to a diverse variety of groups and collectives incorporating governments and executive agencies through to transnational corporations, empowering citizens to supplicate for changes or demand accountability (Cheung, 2019). Petitions are created by individuals or, in the case of change.org, individuals or collectives. To be successful, the petitions necessitate meticulous rumination; thus, gratifying Akram's political participation prerequisites (Akram, 2009). The Gov.uk site was inaugurated in July 2011 following the election of the coalition government. An analogous site was formerly hosted on the Prime Minister's website but was suspended amidst the election, (Connor, 2015). Due to the creation of the government petition sites, several local authorities established petition websites enabling direct democracy locally (Bochel & Bochel, 2016). The current procedure for petitions means petitions in receipt of 10,000 signatures obtain responses from the government and 100,000 signatures mean petitions are considered for debate in the legislature (House of Commons Committee Office, "House of Commons - E-petitions: a collaborative system - Procedure Committee") ,significantly the wording means there is no requisite for petitions to be debated in Parliament and furthermore considerable numbers of petitions breach the terms and conditions. After the inaugural year of the gov.uk petition's site, 47% of petitions had been rejected owing to these conditions (Rath, 2012). The process also denotes that the House of Commons Petitions Committee will elect the means by which to proceed with petitions, meaning many which may reach over

Examining post 2008 youth political participation in the United Kingdom, confirming or questioning the disengaged and disenfranchised consensus?

100,000 signatures will not be debated. Contrasting sharply with Change.org, research from the House of Commons concluded numerous petitions received responses from government departments and MPs without reaching nearly as many signatures. Furthermore, many issues raised on Change.org are debated in Parliament without attaining 100,000 signatures. It remains that Change.org is not a government mandated nor organised site, therefore it could simply be ignored by the government. This is unlikely as it would signify that the government is disregarding one of the most direct and noticeable forms of democratic engagement. The aforementioned issues demonstrate a lack of effectiveness in participation through this means but also indicates occurrences in which they have been extremely successful having received responses and debates (Change.org, "Change.org for parliament ").

Youth participation utilising these tactics is increasingly probable due to the attainability and availability of internet accessibility and literacy within the demographic. Where youth protests may have previously taken place on the streets, nowadays participation can be through the internet with significant results often supported by national and local media coverage, the Local Democracy Reporting Service being an example of local media reporting petitions. Certain issues on petition websites will evidently attract specific age demographics, depending on their nature. Petrov(2014) argues there is a lack of academic consensus surrounding political participation and internet use

Statistics indicate 10% of the UK used the site, (Change.org, "Change.org for parliament ") and a Change.org report for parliament states "Online platforms are more accessible than traditional ways of engaging in [ensuring] that groups that have traditionally been less likely to engage are doing so, such as young people" demonstrating a credence that marginalised collectives are more foreseeably going to participate through un-conventional participation using an E-petition platform. The government has made use of technological innovations in an attempt to reaffirm democracy in addition to improving political participation (Joseph Rowntree Charitable Trust, 2006). Nonetheless there is inconsequential credible nor academic corroboration supporting this as a likely tactic of youth political participation; although democratic innovations such as e-petitions appeal to different models of democracy (Wright, 2012) like those idealised by young people. (Bochel , 2020)suggests an assortment of structural antecedents catalysed the ascension of e-petitions including: declining political engagement, greater need for governmental-citizen interaction, and the advent of the internet. Regardless of this, evidence of mass participation through this method is lacking - only 10.4% people signed petitions in the demographic (Banaji, Buckingham, Van Zoonen, & Hirzalla, 2010), which contrasts to what would conceivably be anticipated within a demographic having typically progressive rates of internet literacy than the broader population. However, there are occasions where young people have successfully used e-petitions as political participation - a 2009 petition initially begun by young people to the Welsh Government resulted in an increased amount of trains running to

Fishbourne (Fox, 2012). However, examples are few and far between and little supports the notion that young people use this as a form of political engagement. In fact (Lindner & Riehm, 2009) several academics propose that introducing democratic innovations such as E-petitions failed to mobilise under-represented groups to partake politically. Upon examining this method of engagement, it becomes clear that E-petitions are rarely a method for engagement and therefore confirms the disengaged and disenfranchised consensus. Data relevant to age demographics using petition sites is inconsiderable and limited, making accurate conclusions difficult; and making these conclusions inevitable but also inconsequential.

Conclusion

Having scrutinised several means of unconventional participation employed by young people in the United Kingdom several conclusions can be drawn, relating to why the methods are used, how effective they are and why they might be chosen over conventional means of participation. Drawing from the aforementioned examples, only certain occurrences have been partially or wholly fruitful, many being unsuccessful or ineffective. Research on aspects of non-conventional political participation is inconclusive or inconsequential especially in relation to examining terrorism and electronic petitions as acts of participation, lesser still was the research looking at the age demographics likely to participate in this participation. The student protests reviewed were unsuccessful in achieving their objectives but attracted significant media attention and therefore held the government to account. Similarly, the strikes were successful.

The 2011 rioting had no clear objectives and had too many motivating factors to be considered a successful act of political engagement. Most of the examples satisfied Akram's (2009) political participation requisites by being considered and organised. Non-conventional participation remains however highly significant often incorporating acts of direct democracy, by those feeling conventional processes have been exhausted or unsuccessful. This may be down to unrepresentative democracy or government, or broken manifesto commitments. Non-conventional participation was primarily found to be as a result of predetermined and already existing democratic interactions through conventional processes and not as an alternate form of engagement. Engagement in unconventional forms of participation is therefore utilised by those already politically engaged through conventional means, an idea substantiated by Petrov (2014) . There is also little evidence to show those involved in unconventional means are not involved in conventional participation. Despite the stereotypes and consensus surrounding youth political engagement, examination of the 16 to 25 age demographic relating to non-conventional participation found limited evidence to suggest that it is a primarily form of engagement in which young people participate over conventional means, finding little to suggest that their rate of involvement through non-conventional means is any higher than

Examining post 2008 youth political participation in the United Kingdom, confirming or questioning the disengaged and disenfranchised consensus?

other age demographics. This chapter demonstrates that although possibly unsuccessful, and no more likely than other demographics, young people are politically engaged through non-conventional means. Inferring they are involved in politics, questioning the aforementioned consensus and stereotype but also allowing the inference that young people remain disenfranchised and disengaged hence using un-conventional means to engage, this notion is dismissed , those engaging unconventionally tend to be ,in tandem , engaged conventionally.

Chapter Two - Examining and Improving Conventional Participation and Associated Issues

Introduction

Conventional participation is circumscribed as participation through traditional democratic processes being voting in elections or referendums. The 16-25 age demographic is alleged to be politically inactive through traditional participation, hence the consensus the demographic is disengaged and disenfranchised. Conventional participation has the altogether more poignant influence on politics as the democratic processes elect the government and legislature therefore non-participation from any demographic presents a predicament, causing these demographics to be marginalized and underrepresented. Note that the age demographic examined in this essay is 16-25 although only over 18s can vote in elections and customarily referendums (except the Scottish independence referendum), the 16-18 demographic was involved in non-conventional participation. The historical context of conventional engagement is heavily linked to the franchise, so is important to examine, to comprehend historical factors which may influence contemporary participation. There remain various motivations which influence voter turnout, evident more so in young people.

Historical Context

The right to free elections is enshrined in article three, protocol one of the European Convention on Human Rights (" European Convention on Human Rights fact sheet", 2016). The franchise in the United Kingdom has an elongated and complex history but is vital to understand historical context in order to comprehend contemporary voter turnout. The United Kingdom maintains what is colloquially known as universal suffrage, those older than 18 may vote irrespective of other factors except incapacity, although concessions remain for this. This has been the case since the 1969 Representation of the People Act. Previously suffrage was introduced piecemeal via various legislative acts gradually extending the franchise. The 1918 Representation of the People Act was the first occasion elections took place on identical days in different constituencies and introduced male suffrage for those above 21 (previously being 25), (Johnston, 2013). The Act meant 74% of the eligible population were registered to vote (Blackburn, 1995). This may perhaps have impacted upon contemporary participation as historically young people were unable to participate owing to legislation.

Elections have been carried out in a democratic manner since the 1832 Reform Act. Previously rotten boroughs meant MPs could be elected by as little as 7 voters under the influence of a regional estate proprietor. Several rotten boroughs elected 2 MPs. (Ertman, 2010), (Pearce, 2004)). Elections are triggered by a dissolution of parliament by royal proclamation thus allowing for election writs to be issued for each constituency. Parliamentary terms run for five years and elections must take place by the end of these. Since the 2011 Fixed Term Parliaments Act parliamentary terms are fixed and elections only called under set conditions. Since 1935, all elections have been held on a Thursday (White & Durkin, 2007) . Electoral processes are overseen by the independent Electoral Commission who appoint returning and presiding officers. In all elections, regional and national returning officers then announce the ballots for candidates in the respective electoral area; constituency, ward or borough. In general elections, a party achieving a majority of seats in the House of Commons is invited by the monarch to form a government. A hung parliament results in a coalition or the forming of a minority government. The electoral process is poignant in understanding youth political engagement through conventional means as it enables the formation of government to be properly examined, therefore exposing the benefits and flaws, these can then be rationalised to view how they influence young people.

Voter turnout, particularly within the youth demographic, has varied but always been rudimentary in comparison to other demographics. Voter turnout increases with age (OECD, 2006). From the 1990s voter turnout has been in decline, peaking in the 1950s with 80% turnout (Uberoi, 2019). Youth voter turnout is ostensibly lower in comparison to other demographics (Gray & Caul, 2000) being the case since the 1960s and widening since the 1990s (Uberoi, 2019). Factors behind a lack of turnout range considerably. Voter absenteeism, registration process, government policy, political socialisation and life pressures are all debated to be contributory factors towards levels of turnout. Academic consensus indicates inequality influences voter turnout (Bartle, Birch & Skirmuntt, 2017). Political discourse generally contends that youth turnout is low, substantiated by British election survey data, reaching its lowest point in 2005 at 38.2% turnout, increasing towards 2017 (Uberoi, 2019). The average UK voter turnout from 1918-2017 was 72.9%. Data demonstrates the high point was in 1964 with youth turnout around 75%. Comparatively the next highest demographic had a turnout of around 80% (Uberoi, 2019). The disparity between the youth age demographic (18-25) and those on the opposite end of the spectrum (65+) is immense. The 1970s had an Eighteen-point turnout gap, 2005 had a Forty point gap and 2010 a Thirty-two point (Birch, Gottfried, & Lodge, 2013) indicating youth participation has been and remains a problem, with no significant upturn

Examining post 2008 youth political participation in the United Kingdom, confirming or questioning the disengaged and disenfranchised consensus?

nor solution in sight. Given the historical context, youth voter turnout is a problem, becoming more so in the contemporary climate. The franchise and context surrounding it is a means of solution but also a factor behind the issue of youth conventional participation.

Methods and Importance of Conventional Participation

Limited methods exist by which individuals may conventionally participate under the definition, local, regional, national and super national elections as the forms of conventional participation and additionally referendums but are typically rarely utilised. However, this trend is fracturing in contemporary history with numerous referendums taking place. Less significant elections also occur; those for the office of the police and crime commissioner and increasingly locally parish and town councils. This essay will focus primarily on national elections with some overview to the relevance of the 2016 referendum in relation to youth conventional participation.

It is difficult to undervalue the nature of conventional participation. As previously stated, it is the method by which the legislature is elected. Despite the various influences on participation through this means, it remains the most used and important form of participation in the contemporary and historical climate. Conventional participation is important as evidence indicates that political parties and associated individuals are more likely to make policies based on those demographics who have high voter turnout (Binstock, 2000). This is seen in the post 2008 climate within the UK. Participation is therefore demonstrably important and substantiates the significance of voter turnout (Fowler, 2013), (Birch, Gottfried , & Lodge, 2013), (Stratmann & Okolski, 2010). Examining turnout rates and youth participation it is evident that it remains a problem which needs to be addressed . The British Social Attitudes Survey states "Younger people are less likely to identify with a political party, less likely to believe it's a civic duty to vote, are less interested in politics and less likely to have undertaken conventional political activities" (" British Social Attitudes", 2013) supporting these concepts.

Post 2008 Conventional Political Participation

Examples

Conventional participation has seen high points in turnout. The 2017 election was broadly christened a "Youth quake" as a result of the vast increase in youth participation, questioning the disengaged and disenfranchised consensus. The then prime minister, Theresa May called the election and the consensus was the election was a forgone conclusion (Sloam & Henn, 2018). The resulting election led to a substantial increase in youth vote and in both Conservative and Labour vote share. Nonetheless the Conservative Party lost 13 seats with a vote share of 42.34%, the Labour Party won an additional 30 seats with a vote share of 39.99%, whilst smaller parties had mixed results (Apostolova, et al., 2019). The election resulted in a hung parliament with no overall majority in the

Examining post 2008 youth political participation in the United Kingdom, confirming or questioning the disengaged and disenfranchised consensus?

legislature and The Conservative Party agreed a confidence and supply arrangement with the Democratic Unionist Party (Tonge, 2017). This is debated to be a result of an increase in youth participation, evidencing the impact that conventional youth political participation may have. Bruter & Harrison,("EU referendum: breaking indifference") contends that young people have been more engaged since the EU referendum. Research for the House of Commons indicates overall turnout was 69% and youth turnout (18-25) was 64 %. Notably this was not the lowest demographic for turnout - the 35-44 age demographic had a turnout of 63% and youth turnout was up by 20% compared to the 2015 election (Apostolova, et al., 2019). Academics (Simpson & Curtice, 2018) contend that levels of youth turnout increased to an extent that had not been seen since the 1990s demonstrating that despite the consensus that young people are not disengaged and disenfranchised this is not necessarily the case, not being the lowest demographic and the turnout is increasing. The youth vote was considerably important in this election, 31 seats were held or gained with a margin of under one percent , five of these by 30 votes or less (McInnes, 2019) - the high youth turnout secured some of these seats. Hypothetically an even more marked increase in youth turnout may have seen altogether different election results. Had youth participation been equal to the over 65s with the same voter preferences as their peers, between 5-10 seats would have moved from Conservative to Labour (Barford, 2017), although there is no collaboration between the safeness of seats and voter turnout as a higher turnout may result in more seats changing parties. The home counties including Kent have been traditionally staunchly conservative (Warren, 2017) but in 2017 the Kent constituency of Canterbury was a Labour gain after over a century of Conservative representation. Young voters are credited with supporting this gain (Chakelian, 2019). Gamble contests that "The surge of young voters ... saw the capture of traditional Conservative seats including Kensington and Canterbury." (Gamble, 2018) and supports that the increase in youth vote supported a shift in the long-held seats, not just traditional marginals or bellwether seats.

Youth participation was evident though the increased turnout and associated effects this caused. The increase in participation and consequentially, turnout, can be suggested to have been caused by a range of factors including political parties targeting young voters, specifically the Labour, Green and Liberal Democrat parties with certain key policies impacting young people. While the Conservative party also did this, these policies were not framed as benefitting young people and were limited in effectiveness of targeting the demographic (Sloam & Henn, 2018). Young people were more likely to use online media platforms and social media during the election than other demographics, being effectively utilised by the aforementioned parties to target younger demographics. Labour leader Jeremy Corbyn had a social media following across platforms of 1,400,000 in comparison to Conservative leader Theresa May's 439,000. (Sloam, Ehsan, & Henn, 2018) , (Sloam & Henn, 2018). Some argue this presents a decline in democracy (Crouch, 2017).

Examining post 2008 youth political participation in the United Kingdom, confirming or questioning the disengaged and disenfranchised consensus?

Left-wing political group Momentum employed tactics similar to the Sander's American presidential campaign in order to galvanise the youth vote ("Inside Momentum's campaign 'hackathon'", 2017). Momentum used a hybridisation of contemporary and traditional campaign tactics to target the youth demographic including texting over emailing and going door to door and using apps (Zagoria, Schulkind, & Zagoria, 2017) and was successful in the mobilisation of the youth vote. Momentum supported the Labour Party (Middleton, 2018), therefore targeting the youth demographic whom were more likely to vote for the Labour Party and left wing (Sturgis & Jennings, 2020). The efforts it put into improving youth turnout may have had repercussions for the turnout as a whole. Organisations such as Grime4Corbyn and Momentum's wider digital strategy in both digital media and traditional campaigning worked in tandem to boost youth turnout (Dommett & Temple, 2018). Although these strategies had opportunities to do more, it is substantially evident that the methods used were effective and amongst other factors may have supported Labour's appeal to younger demographics (Whiteley, Poletti, Webb, & Bale, 2018). Other celebrity fronted campaigns supported both registration and turnout (Wolfson, 2017) and as a result from the surprising result of the 2016 EU referendum, (Pearce & Fox, 2016) Sloam & Henn (2018) state it "had a clear positive impact on young people's political engagement".

39   Examining post 2008 youth political participation in the United Kingdom, confirming or questioning the disengaged and disenfranchised consensus?

Summarising the 2017 election it is noticeable that through a range of factors, young people were increasingly likely to turn out and vote and this had poignant impacts both in terms of vote share and in terms of seats, more so had turnout increased further. Many long held and traditionally safe seats changed parties due to the increase in youth participation. The substantial uptake in engagement dismisses the notion that young people are disengaged or disenfranchised substantiating the fact that the youth demographic is more engaged than it previously has been and the decline in participation is now on an upward trajectory.

The lowest ebb of youth political engagement since 2008 occurred in 2015 with a youth turnout of 43%. Comparatively the general population had a turnout of 66%. 2010 had similar results with a youth turnout of 44% and overall turnout of 65%. The similarity between these elections would indicate no factors influencing turnout although not necessarily the case. Several factors influenced youth turnout. The influence of a lack of voter turnout may have allowed both the coalition to be elected and the 2015 Conservative government. Increased youth participation would have ensured these elections were representative, with youth turnout levels lower than the general population neither election can be considered representative. During this period both the Coalition and Conservative government enacted a socio-economic policy of austerity and most cuts were proven to have impacted young people as well as other disengaged demographics owing to the lower turnout with these demographics as some academics have suggested. The importance of youth turnout is

Examining post 2008 youth political participation in the United Kingdom, confirming or questioning the disengaged and disenfranchised consensus?

demonstrated, as the demographic with a low turnout was hit hardest by cuts whilst the demographic which had the highest turnout, the over 65s, was less impacted substantiating the theory that had youth turnout been equally substantial as the over 65s, the government's policies' may have been less damaging to the demographic. In the broader context, youth turnout would have ensured the government both accounted for the demographic and was representative of them when creating and enacting policies.

The low youth turnout is debated to have been caused by several factors; voter registration, apathy with politics and alienation as well as voting taking too much time. Academics present the argument that students could have swayed the result of the 2015 election with the caveat that to do so they would have to register and turnout (Burns, 2014), The majority of those impacted by changes to voter registration were young and between 800 thousand to a million people were left off the electoral roll as a result of these changes (Morris, 2015) , (Wheeler, 2015). Apathy and alienation also play a part in poor turnouts at both elections, which is contended as a reason young people don't participate (Dahl, et al., 2017). Fox supports this argument but contends this is only applicable for participation and not the case in non-conventional participation. (Fox, 2015).

It is evident that the low turnout from the youth demographic meant they were negatively impacted by government agendas during this period.

41 Examining post 2008 youth political participation in the United Kingdom, confirming or questioning the disengaged and disenfranchised consensus?

Austerity adversely impacted demographics with low turnout, not just the youth but across the board, demonstrating a major problem with a lack of participation through conventional means. Lack of participation means a lack of representation , negatively influences the demographic. The turnout in both these elections was low compared to the wider population. The aforementioned factors give some indication of the reasons behind this. Youth participation may be increased by resolving issues with voter registration by introducing automatic or compulsory registration. The turnout at both these elections adheres to the stereotypical view that youth are both disengaged and disenfranchised, especially given the context of the wider population.

The EU referendum in 2016 is unique, being the only post 2008 form of conventional political participation, not being an election. The results were widely deemed a forgone conclusion but, surprisingly to political commentators, polling organisations and politicians themselves, the Leave campaign won. Polling contends that most individuals within the 16-25 demographic supported the Remain campaign which lost thereby demonstrating participation as important.

Youth turnout in the referendum was 64% (Helm, 2016), high in comparison to elections supporting the theory that young people are not disengaged and disenfranchised in terms of conventional political participation. The turnout may be a result of every vote counting in referendums unlike elections. Other factors include the use of social media and political marketing (Pich, et al., 2018) , the idea of group collaboration and increased knowledge about the issue (Sloam, 2018). Bruter states young people "find it easier to get passionate about an issue than … a party" thus demonstrating a reasoning behind the explosive increase in youth participation at the referendum, which carried through to the 2017 election. Hix and Marsh (2007) imply European elections are used to punish national governments , and the EU referendum can be seen to be a result of this , hence the increase in turnout.

This had an impact on future youth participation - the turnout from the youth demographic increased as a result of the EU referendum's shock result pushing many individuals from various demographics to turnout and vote in future elections and referendums. Remains' loss in the referendum indicated that young people's voices still counted and were crucial in the political arena. Many viewed this as a critical turning point for conventional participation going on to encourage young people to utilise their vote. Young people voting in the Referendum for the first time were thereby increasingly likely to vote in future elections as the formation of a political habit, those who vote when first eligible and during political socialisation are more likely to turn out and vote (Grönlund & Milner, 2006).

The EU referendum substantiates that young people are increasingly political engaged and not disenfranchised. The marked increase in participation demonstrates the demographic to be highly mobile in terms of political participation. The referendum was however unique. Using technology in the campaign was a factor which now remains pertinent in all elections, especially after the referendum, allowing specific targeting of demographics.

Conclusion

Examining the post 2008 elections and the referendum youth turnout since 2008 is mixed. Immediately after 2008 the turnout remained poor and stagnant, whilst 2017 appears to demonstrate a turning point with a marked increase in youth engagement through conventional means. However, the many factors behind this mean it may not be the new norm although indicating a substantial increase in turnout which may mean turnout has improved in comparison from previous years. Early figures relating to the 2019 election prove that this may not remain the case as turnout here was 47 % in the youth age group against national average turnout of 67% (McInnes, 2020). Future youth turnout perhaps cannot be guaranteed nor estimated to be in decline or increasing, and needs addressing in order to ensure democracy in the UK remains representative for all demographics.

Factors influencing conventional participation and solutions to increase the youth conventional political participation.

Several factors have impacted youth conventional participation. The Electoral Commission presents a list of primary factors which are cited as the main reasons why young people don't vote; " disillusion… , apathy…,individual impact … , alienation… , lack of knowledge … and

Examining post 2008 youth political participation in the United Kingdom, confirming or questioning the disengaged and disenfranchised consensus?

inconvenience .... " (The Electoral Commission, 2002). These factors can be easily solved through a number of solutions in order to increase turnout and conventional participation. Increasing political and citizenship education (Milligan, Moretti, & Oreopoulos, 2004) has been proven to increase voting rates and political engagement, increasing public relations campaigns to counteract disillusion, apathy and the belief that individual impact doesn't matter – constituencies can be gained or lost on very few votes, and improvements to voting method such as longer polling day, or more polling days, online voting or more promotion of proxy voting. These would counter many of the key reasons people choose not to vote but alone may not be enough to increase conventional participation.

Academic research suggests that amendments to the voter registration process had adverse impacts on youth turnout, supporting the idea that young people are disenfranchised. Before the 2015 election the legal emphasis for registration moved from householder to individuals. This transition is widely refuted to have overtly impacted the youth demographic (Fisher & Hillman, 2014) , particularly, transient populations such as students due to the way the change was rolled out resulting in an estimated 1 million voters coming off the electoral roll, meaning these voters could not participate. Many of these were young people ((Wintour, 2015)). After the 2015 election it was contended that going forward another 7 million people would drop off the electoral roll once again mostly impacting students. The move from household to individual voter registration resulted in a 90% drop in registration in university residences (Wheeler, 2015). Another reason can be avoidance of registration relating to secondary utilisation of the register. The register can be used for a vast number of things including marketing, credit checks and background checks by both governments and private employers ("The Representation of the People (England and Wales) (Description of Electoral Registers and Amendment) Regulations 2013"). These reasons may discourage some people from registering (The Electoral Commission, 2002) however little supports this solely relates to examining youth registration.

One often touted solution to improving youth turnout in elections which would also ensure smoother registration would be the introduction of compulsory voting and/or registration, which would ensure near universal turnout (Kouba & Mysicka, 2019). This presents numerous issues with some viewing this measure as draconian and vying it makes democracy less representative as people are forced to make a choice (Umbers, 2018). The justification is that the current scenario leaves a significant minority without a voice, albeit by choice. To ensure that this solution would be effective, safeguards would need to be put in place, allowing for proxy votes, spoilt ballots or none of the above options on the ballot paper. Compulsory voting could be easily introduced within the parameters of the existing system and could be enforced by means of a small fine so as not to adversely affect those who still abstain. Compulsory registration could be done through the same method and enforcement but would need safeguards too around secondary uses of the electoral roll much like current safeguards for the open register. These two solutions would be highly effective but could limit the freedoms of individuals (Volacu, 2019) and thus need to be carefully considered and only used as an option of last resort to improve participation.

Chapter Three – Conclusions

Having examined multiple forms of political engagement, both conventional and unconventional, young people in the United Kingdom since 2008 are not politically disengaged or disenfranchised but are less engaged through conventional participation often employing unconventional forms of political engagement in order to achieve objectives, despite not always being successful. As suggested by bang and Sorensen (2004) bounders are blurred and participation now concerns broader ranging issues and methods, Unconventional participation in the youth demographic since 2008 rarely employed illegal tactics except for the rioting ,which had numerous factors motivating it and was not purely political.

Successful use of unconventional political engagement by the youth demographic held the government to account in relation to the increase in tuition fees. Conventional participation also held the government to account at the subsequent election, however as mentioned this is often too slow to have significant political repercussions. Other forms of unconventional participation have limited studies to show their effectiveness or the motivations for using these tactics, however, the research that is available demonstrates that young people will still utilise these means, such as petitions even if not conventionally engaged but those that participate through these means are more likely to already be engaged in conventional forms. Overall unconventional political participation in the youth age group remains incredibly important as an outlet for political actions when other avenues have been exhausted or have failed, meaning it can be seen as a tool for those who feel apathetic but also demonstrates that young people remain politically engaged not just during election periods and that political engagement is more than just voting to young people especially when it relates to issues pertinent to them. Taking the EU referendum and the student protests as examples, we can see that young people appear to be far more passionate about specific issues than about wider politics, and this can influence their political engagement on a number of levels.

Engagement through conventional means has had varying degrees of participation influenced by the issues surrounding the elections and the perception of whether young votes will count. Since 2008, the youth turnout began at a low. Although 2015 had a lower youth turnout than 2010 ,both were markedly lower than the 2016 referendum and 2017

Examining post 2008 youth political participation in the United Kingdom, confirming or questioning the disengaged and disenfranchised consensus?

election. The referendum changed the way individual votes were perceived and mobilised youth conventional participation. Alongside this, several other factors influenced youth voter registration. The celebrity and social media campaigns had a positive impact by supporting a higher registration and turnout in both the referendum and the 2017 election. The 2017 election evidences clearly the role young people play in politics and they are neither disengaged or disenfranchised. Despite having comparatively lower turnouts to the wider population or the demographic with the highest turnout, the over 65s, youth turnout since 2008 has always been equal to or greater than 43%. This is a significant minority, whilst below average by around 20%. In 2016 and 2017 the turnout was much closer to the population average, meaning youth turnout cannot always be predicated or relied upon as a measure of youth political engagement but remains an important nonetheless.

A mixture of both conventional and non-conventional participation substantiates that young people have been and remain politically engaged since 2008 but poor turnout in conventional participation meant that young people have been stereotyped as being disengaged and disenfranchised . There is still room for significant improvements, which would increase youth political turnout and conventional participation. The most effective but also most controversial would be compulsory voting yet other smaller and more reasonable solutions would also be impactful in increasing youth conventional participation including changes to registration process and increased awareness campaigning surrounding the importance of voting. These measures would support the participation across all marginalised demographics and not just the youth demographic which would arguably be for the broader good leading to a more representative democracy.

Bibliography

Abrahams, J., & Brooks, R. (2018). Higher education students as political actors: evidence from England and Ireland. *Journal of Youth Studies*, *22*(1), 108–123. doi: 10.1080/13676261.2018.1484431

Akram. (2014). *Handbook of youth and young adulthood: new perspectives and agendas pg.213 -229*. Place of publication not identified: Routledge.

Akram, S. (2014). Recognizing the 2011 United Kingdom Riots as Political Protest. *British Journal of Criminology*, *54*(3), 375–392. doi: 10.1093/bjc/azu013

Almond, G. A., & Verba, S. (1963). The Civic Culture. *Center for International Studies*. doi: 10.1515/9781400874569

Apostolova, Audickas, Baker, Bate, Cracknell, Dempsey, ... Uberoi. (2019). *General Election 2017: results and analysis* (2nd ed.). London: Parliament.

Appian . (n.d.). The Histories of Appian ,THE CIVIL WARS Book I. Retrieved January 19, 2020, from https://penelope.uchicago.edu/Thayer/E/Roman/Texts/Appian/Civil_Wars/1*.html

Banaji, Buckingham, Van Zoonen, & Hirzalla. (2010). *Synthesis of CivicWeb results and policy outcomes*. london: institute of Education.

Bang, H. P., & Sørensen, E. P. (2014). The Everyday Maker. *Social Capital and Participation in Everyday Life*, 148–161. doi: 10.4324/9780203451571_chapter_11

Barentsen, J. (2013). From disaffected consumer to opportunistic looter? *International Journal of Adolescence and Youth*, *18*(2), 65–68. doi: 10.1080/02673843.2013.806429

Barford, V. (2017, May 19). Election 2017: If more young people actually voted, would it change everything? Retrieved March 24, 2020, from https://www.bbc.co.uk/news/election-2017-39965925

Barrett, M., & Brunton-Smith, I. (2017). Political and Civic Engagement and Participation: Towards an Integrative Perspective. *Framing Civic Engagement, Political Participation and Active Citizenship in Europe*, 5–28. doi: 10.4324/9781315738260-2

Bartle, J., Birch, S., & Skirmuntt, M. (2017). The local roots of the participation gap: Inequality and voter turnout. *Electoral Studies*, *48*, 30–44. doi: 10.1016/j.electstud.2017.05.004

Bendix, R., & Huntington, S. P. (1971). Political Order in Changing Societies. *Political Science Quarterly*, *86*(1), 168. doi: 10.2307/2147388

Berger, B. (2009). Political Theory, Political Science and the End of Civic Engagement. *Perspectives on Politics*, *7*(2), 335–350. doi: 10.1017/s153759270909080x

Berman, G. (2014). *The August 2011 riots: a statistical summary* (SG, Vol. SN). westminster, London: Parliment, House of Commons.

Bertsou. (2019). Political Distrust and its Discontents: Exploring the Meaning, Expression and Significance of Political Distrust. *Societies, 9*(4), 72. doi: 10.3390/soc9040072

Biggs, M., & Knauss, S. (2011). Explaining Membership in the British National Party: A Multilevel Analysis of Contact and Threat. *European Sociological Review, 28*(5), 633–646. doi: 10.1093/esr/jcr031

Biggs, M. (2015, April 4). The causes and consequences of the 2011 London riots. Retrieved February 10, 2020, from https://blog.oup.com/2015/03/social-forces-london-riots/

Binstock, R. (2000). Older people and voting participation: past and future. *The Gerontologist, 40*(1), 18–31. doi: 10.1093/geront/40.1.18

Birch, S., Gottfried , G., & Lodge, G. (2013). *Divided democracy - Political Inequality In The Uk And Why It Matters*. London: Institute for Public Policy Research.

Blackburn, R. (1995). *The electoral system in Britain*. Basingstoke: Macmillan.

Blais, A. (2000). To Vote or Not to Vote. doi: 10.2307/j.ctt5hjrrf

Blick, A. (2015). Constitutional Implications of the Fixed-Term Parliaments Act 2011. *Parliamentary Affairs*, *69*(1), 19–35. doi: 10.1093/pa/gsv004

Bochel, C., & Bochel, H. (2016). 'Reaching in'? The potential for e-petitions in local government in the United Kingdom. *Information, Communication & Society*, *20*(5), 683–699. doi: 10.1080/1369118x.2016.1203455

Bochel , C. (2020). petitions Systems: Outcomes, 'Success' and 'Failure' . *Parliamentary Affairs*, *73*(2), 233–252.

Boon, M. (2010). *Understanding the rise of the far right: Survey results.* Manchester, Greater Manchester: Equality and Human Rights Commission.

Brady, H. E., Verba, S., & Schlozman, K. L. (1995). Beyond SES: A Resource Model of Political Participation. *American Political Science Review, 89*(2), 271–294. doi: 10.2307/2082425

Brady, H. E., Schlozman, K. L., & Verba, S. (1999). Prospecting for Participants: Rational Expectations and the Recruitment of Political Activists. *American Political Science Review, 93*(1), 153–168. doi: 10.2307/2585767

Bridges, L. (2012). Four days in August: the UK riots. *Race & Class, 54*(1), 1–12. doi: 10.1177/0306396812446564

NatCen Social Research. (2013). *British Social Attitudes.* London.

Bruter , & Harrison. (n.d.). EU referendum: breaking indifference. Retrieved April 4, 2020, from http://www.lse.ac.uk/about-lse/connect/connect-2017/eu-referendum-breaking-indifference

Burns, J. (2014, December 1). Student vote could swing 2015 election, suggests study. Retrieved February 3, 2020, from https://www.bbc.co.uk/news/education-30252713

Cant, C., & Woodcock, J. (2020). Fast Food Shutdown: From disorganisation to action in the service sector. *Capital & Class*, 030981682090635. doi: 10.1177/0309816820906357

Carpini, M. X. D. (2000). Gen.com: Youth, Civic Engagement, and the New Information Environment. *Political Communication, 17*(4), 341–349. doi: 10.1080/10584600050178942

Chakelian, A. (2019, November 25). Could Remain pain in Canterbury cost Labour its only seat in Kent? Retrieved March 2, 2020, from https://www.newstatesman.com/politics/uk/2019/11/remain-pact-alliance-Brexit-Lib-Dems-Labour-canterbury-only-seat-kent

Change.org. (n.d.). *Change.org for parliament* . San Francisco, California: Chnage.org.

Chapman, B. (2019, November 12). McDonald's staff go on strike and march on Downing Street demanding better pay. Retrieved from https://www.independent.co.uk/news/business/news/mcdonalds-strike-today-mcstrike-higher-pay-downing-street-john-mcdonnell-a9199681.html

Chapman, B. (2018, January 4). McDonald's staff are getting a pay rise after strikes. Retrieved February 10, 2020, from https://www.independent.co.uk/news/business/news/mcdonalds-worker-pay-rise-wages-strike-bakers-union-fast-food-restaurant-a8141151.html

Cheung, H. (2019, March 26). Brexit debate: Do petitions ever work? Retrieved May 1, 2020, from https://www.bbc.co.uk/news/world-47693506

Clark, W. (2018). *Activism in the public sphere: exploring the discourse of political participation*. London: Routledge.

Clarke, K. (2011, September 5). Punish the feral rioters, but address our social deficit too. Retrieved May 16, 2020, from https://www.theguardian.com/commentisfree/2011/sep/05/punishment-rioters-help

Connor, G. (2015, October 30). Are e-petitions a waste of time? Retrieved May 1, 2020, from https://www.bbc.co.uk/news/uk-politics-34476264

Conway, M. M. (2000). *Political participation in the United States*. Washington, D.C.: CQ Press.

Crouch, C. (2017). *Post-democracy*. Cambridge: Polity Press.

Crown prosecution service - Terrorism. (2020, February 29). Retrieved May 16, 2020, from https://www.cps.gov.uk/terrorism

Cutts, D., & Russell, A. (2015). From Coalition to Catastrophe: The Electoral Meltdown of the Liberal Democrats. *Parliamentary Affairs, 68*(suppl 1), 70–87. doi: 10.1093/pa/gsv028

Dahl, R. A. (1989). *Democarcy and its critics*. New Haven: Yale Univ. Press.

Dahl, V., Amnå, E., Banaji, S., Landberg, M., Šerek, J., Ribeiro, N., ... Zani, B. (2017). Apathy or alienation? Political passivity among youths across eight European Union countries. *European Journal of Developmental Psychology*, *15*(3), 284–301. doi: 10.1080/17405629.2017.1404985

Dalton, R. J. (2008). Citizenship Norms and the Expansion of Political Participation. *Political Studies*, *56*(1), 76–98. doi: 10.1111/j.1467-9248.2007.00718.x

Darden, J. T. (2019). *Tackling Terrorists' Exploitation of Youth* . Washington , District of Columbia: American Enterprise Institute .

Department for Communities and Local Government . (2013). *Government Response to the Riots, Communities and Victims Panel's final report* . westminster, london: Department for Communities and Local Government .

Deželan Tomaž, & Lisney, J. (2015). *Young people and democratic life in Europe: what next after the 2014 European elections?* Brussels: European Youth Forum.

Dommett, K., & Temple, L. (2018). Digital Campaigning: The Rise of Facebook and Satellite Campaigns. *Parliamentary Affairs, 71*(suppl_1), 189–202. doi: 10.1093/pa/gsx056

Ekman, J., & Amnå, E. (2012). Political participation and civic engagement: Towards a new typology. *Human Affairs, 22*(3). doi: 10.2478/s13374-012-0024-1

Ertman, T. (2010). The Great Reform Act of 1832 and British Democratization. *Comparative Political Studies, 43*(8-9), 1000–1022. doi: 10.1177/0010414010370434

ECHR. European Convention on Human Rights fact sheet, European Convention on Human Rights fact sheet (2016). Strasbourg.

European union . (n.d.). Glossary on youth. Retrieved May 4, 2020, from https://pjp-eu.coe.int/en/web/youth-partnership/glossary

FAQS: McDonald's UK. (n.d.). Retrieved May 17, 2020, from

https://www.mcdonalds.com/gb/en-gb/help/faq/18338-what-is-the-average-age-of-a-mcdonalds-employee.html

Farthing, R. (2010, February 25). The politics of youthful antipolitics: representing the 'issue' of youth participation in politics. Retrieved May 16, 2020, from https://www.tandfonline.com/doi/full/10.1080/13676260903233696?casa_token=6AY7ycWsyoIAAAAA:kVbFF_lCyQJYuyWZWfIRbQhuUngxgmGVOkHPHP4z8ReXQyeDjEvfJDvKIdTV_vT8ksZrSmwi8Q

Finch, G., Verba, S., & Nie, N. H. (1974). Participation in America: Political Democracy and Social Equality. *Political Science Quarterly*, *89*(3), 674. doi: 10.2307/2148474

Fisher, & Hillman. (2014). *Do students swing elections? Registration, turnout and voting behaviour among full-time students*. Oxford: HEPI.

Flatley, J. (2019). *Operation of police powers under the Terrorism Act 2000 and subsequent legislation: Arrests, outcomes, and stop and search, Great Britain, financial year ending March 2019.* Home office / Office for National Statistics. Retrieved from https://assets.publishing.service.gov.uk/government/uploads/system/uploads/attachment_data/file/808190/police-powers-terrorism-mar2019-hosb0819.pdf

Flint, J., & Powell, R. (2012). The English City Riots of 2011, 'Broken Britain' and the Retreat into the Present. *Sociological Research Online, 17*(3), 153–162. doi: 10.5153/sro.2748

Forbrig, J. (2005). *Revisiting youth political participation: challenges for research and democratic practice in Europe.* Strasbourg: Council of Europe Pub.

Fowler, A. (2013). *Five Studies on the Causes and Consequences of Voter Turnout* (dissertation). Harvard University, Cambridge, MA.

Fox, R. (2012). *What next for e-petitions?* London: The Hansard Societ.

Fox, S. (2015). *Apathy, alienation and young people: the political engagement of British millennials* (dissertation). University of Nottingham, Nottingham.

Furlong, A., & Cartmel, F. (2007). *Young people and social change: new perspectives*. Maidenhead: McGraw-Hill/Open University Press.

Furlong, A. (Ed.). (2014). *Handbook of youth and young adulthood: new perspectives and agendas*. Routledge.

Gamble, A. (2018). Taking back control: the political implications of Brexit. *Journal of European Public Policy, 25*(8), 1215–1232. doi: 10.1080/13501763.2018.1467952

Gilroy, P. (2002). *The cultural politics of race and nation*. London: Routledge.

Gould, A. M. (2010). Working at McDonalds: some redeeming features of McJobs. *Work, Employment and Society, 24*(4), 780–802. doi: 10.1177/0950017010380644

Greenwood, L. (2011, August 20). England riots: Debate over clean-up costs. Retrieved May 16, 2020, from https://www.bbc.co.uk/news/business-14590252

Grönlund, K., & Milner, H. (2006). The Determinants of Political Knowledge in Comparative Perspective. *Scandinavian Political Studies*, *29*(4), 386–406. doi: 10.1111/j.1467-9477.2006.00157.x

Grönlund, K., & Milner, H. (2006). The Determinants of Political Knowledge in Comparative Perspective. *Scandinavian Political Studies*, *29*(4), 386–406. doi: 10.1111/j.1467-9477.2006.00157.x

Górecki, M. A. (2013). Election Closeness, Habit Formation and Voter Turnout: Evidence from Sixteen Swedish Elections. *Political Studies*, *61*(1_suppl), 234–248. doi: 10.1111/1467-9248.12017

Hay, C. (2007). *Why We Hate Politics*. Cambridge: Polity press.

Helm, T. (2016, July 10). EU referendum: youth turnout almost twice as high as first thought. Retrieved May 14, 2020, from https://www.theguardian.com/politics/2016/jul/09/young-people-referendum-turnout-brexit-twice-as-high

Henn, M., & Foard, N. (2011). Young People, Political Participation and Trust in Britain. *Parliamentary Affairs, 65*(1), 47–67. doi: 10.1093/pa/gsr046

Henn, M., & Oldfield, B. (2016). Cajoling or coercing: would electoral engineering resolve the young citizen–state disconnect? *Journal of Youth Studies, 19*(9), 1259–1280. doi: 10.1080/13676261.2016.1154935

Hensby, A. (2017). *Participation and non-participation in student activism. Paths and barriers to mobilising young people for political action.* unknown: Rowman & Littlefield Publ.

Hibbing, J. R., & Theiss-Morse, E. (2002). *Stealth democracy: americans beliefs about how government should work.* Cambridge: University.

Highton, B. (2009). Revisiting the Relationship between Educational Attainment and Political Sophistication. *The Journal of Politics, 71*(4), 1564–1576. doi: 10.1017/s0022381609990077

Hillman, N. (2016). The Coalition's higher education reforms in England. *Oxford Review of Education, 42*(3), 330–345. doi: 10.1080/03054985.2016.1184870

Hix, S., & Marsh, M. (2007). Punishment or Protest? Understanding European Parliament Elections. *The Journal of Politics, 69*(2), 495–510. doi: 10.1111/j.1468-2508.2007.00546.x

House of Commons Committee Office. (n.d.). House of Commons - E-petitions: a collaborative system - Procedure Committee. Retrieved April 13, 2020, from https://publications.parliament.uk/pa/cm201415/cmselect/cmproced/235/23506.htm

Inside Momentum's campaign 'hackathon'. (2017, August 7). Retrieved May 17, 2020, from https://www.bbc.co.uk/news/av/uk-politics-40850882/inside-momentum-s-campaign-hackathon

Jahoda, M. (1982). *Employment and unemployment: a social-psychological analysis*. Cambridge, Angleterre: Cambridge University Press.

Johnston, neil. (2013). *The History of the Parliamentary Franchise*. wesminster: Parliament, House of commons.

Jones, O. (2018, October 4). Young people are rewiring capitalism with their McStrike | Owen Jones. Retrieved April 2, 2020, from https://www.theguardian.com/commentisfree/2018/oct/04/young-people-capitalism-mcstrike-unions

Joseph Rowntree Charitable Trust. (2006). *Power to the people: the report of Power: an independent inquiry into Britains democracy*. york: York Publishing.

Kaid, L. L., Mckinney, M. S., & Tedesco, J. C. (2007). Political Information Efficacy and Young Voters. *American Behavioral Scientist, 50*(9), 1093–1111. doi: 10.1177/0002764207300040

Kaid, L. L., Mckinney, M. S., & Tedesco, J. C. (2007). Introduction: Political Information Efficacy and Young Voters. *American Behavioral Scientist, 50*(9), 1093–1111. doi: 10.1177/0002764207300040

Karbach, & Pleyers. (2014). *Young people political participation in Europe: What do we mean by participation?* Brussels : Unknown.

Keeter, S., Zukin, cliff, Andolina, M., & Jenkins, K. (2002). *The Civic and Political Health of the Nation: A Generational Portrait.* New Brunswick, New Jersey: Rutgers Universit.

Keith, M. (1993). *Race, riots and policing: lore and disorder in a multi-racist society.* London: UCL Press.

Kelsey, D., Mueller, F., Whittle, A., & Khosravinik, M. (2015). Financial crisis and austerity: interdisciplinary concerns in critical discourse studies. *Critical Discourse Studies, 13*(1), 1–19. doi: 10.1080/17405904.2015.1074600

Kirk-Wade, E., & Allen, G. (2020). *Terrorism in Great Britain: the statistics.* westminster, london: Parliament , House of commons library .

Kollewe, J., & Slawson, N. (2017, September 4). McDonald's workers to go on strike in Britain for first time. Retrieved March 11, 2020, from https://www.theguardian.com/business/2017/sep/04/mcdonalds-workers-strike-cambridge-crayford

Kouba, K., & Mysicka, S. (2019). Should and Does Compulsory Voting Reduce Inequality? *SAGE Open*, *9*(1), 215824401881714. doi: 10.1177/2158244018817141

Kumar, A. (2011). *"Did Anything Change?" Evaluating the Effectiveness of the 2010 UK Student Protests* (dissertation). London School of Economics and Political Science, London.

Lewis, P., Adegoke, Y., & Burch, A. (2012). *Reading the riots: investigating Englands summer of disorder*. London: Guardian.

Lindner, R., & Riehm, U. (2009). Electronic Petitions and Institutional Modernization. International Parliamentary E-Petition Systems in Comparative Perspective. *JeDEM - EJournal of EDemocracy and Open Government*, *1*(1), 1–11. doi: 10.29379/jedem.v1i1.3

Longo, & Meyer. (2006). *College Students and Politics: A Literature Review*. Medford, Massachusetts: center for information and research on civic learning and engagement.

Mampaey, J., Wit, K. D., & Broucker, B. (2019). The delegitimation of student protest against market-oriented reforms in higher education: the role of mass media discourse. *Studies in Higher Education*, 1–11. doi: 10.1080/03075079.2019.1643304

Manning, N. (2010). Tensions in Young Peoples Conceptualisation and Practice of Politics. *Sociological Research Online*, *15*(4), 55–64. doi: 10.5153/sro.2256

MARSH, D. (2016). *Young People And Politics In The Uk: apathy or alienation?* Place of publication not identified: PALGRAVE MACMILLAN.

McElwee, S. (2015, October 19). Why Increasing Voter Turnout Affects Policy. Retrieved March 25, 2020, from https://www.theatlantic.com/politics/archive/2015/09/why-non-voters-matter/405250/

McInnes, R. (2019, August 19). GE2017: Marginal seats and turnout. Retrieved March 22, 2020, from https://commonslibrary.parliament.uk/insights/ge2017-marginal-seats-and-turnout/

McInnes, R. (2020, January 8). General Election 2019: Turnout. Retrieved April 18, 2020, from https://commonslibrary.parliament.uk/insights/general-election-2019-turnout/

Middleton, A. (2018). 'For the Many, Not the Few': Strategising the Campaign Trail at the 2017 UK General Election. *Parliamentary Affairs*, *72*(3), 501–521. doi: 10.1093/pa/gsy034

Milligan, K., Moretti, E., & Oreopoulos, P. (2004). Does education improve citizenship? Evidence from the United States and the United Kingdom. *Journal of Public Economics*, *88*(9-10), 1667–1695. doi: 10.1016/j.jpubeco.2003.10.005

Moran, M., & Waddington, D. (2016). *Riots An International Comparison*. London: Palgrave Macmillan UK.

Moran, M. (2006, March 16). Terrorist Groups and Political Legitimacy. Retrieved from https://www.cfr.org/backgrounder/terrorist-groups-and-political-legitimacy

Most young lack interest in politics - official survey. (2014, February 21). Retrieved May 2, 2020, from https://www.bbc.co.uk/news/uk-politics-26271935

Murugesu, J. (2017, September 4). McStrike: Why McDonald's staff are taking to the picket line. Retrieved March 17, 2020, from https://www.newstatesman.com/politics/economy/2017/09/mcstrike-why-mcdonalds-staff-are-taking-picket-line

Neligan, myles. (2011, August 11). Riots to cost over £200 million - ABI. Retrieved May 16, 2020, from https://uk.reuters.com/article/uk-britain-riots-cost/riots-to-cost-over-200-million-abi-idUKTRE77A22H20110811

Nigel Morris. (2015, April 17). Democracy is in crisis as the numbers of registered voters has dropped by over 800,000. Retrieved from https://www.independent.co.uk/news/uk/politics/generalelection/general-election-2015-huge-drop-in-registered-voters-could-have-crucial-impact-on-who-forms-next-10183061.html

Norris, P. (2003). Preaching to the Converted? *Party Politics*, *9*(1), 21–45. doi: 10.1177/135406880391003

Nowak, P., & Hodder, A. (2019). 150 years of the Trades Union Congress – reflections on the past and challenges for the future. *Employee Relations*, *41*(2), 270–278. doi: 10.1108/er-12-2018-0323

Ogris, G., & Westphal, S. (Eds.). (2005). *Political Participation of Young People in Europe – Development of Indicators for Comparative Research in the European Union (Euyoupart)* (Vol. 17). Vienna: SORA.

Organisation for Economic Cooperation and Developmen. (2006). Society at a Glance 2006: OECD Social Indicators. Retrieved May 17, 2020, from https://www.oecd-ilibrary.org/social-issues-migration-health/society-at-a-glance-2006_soc_glance-2006-en

Owen, D., Green, A., kik, G., Luanaigh, A. ni, Greevy, H., Morrice, N., & Robertson, kyle. How has the UK Restaurant sector been affected by the fissuring of the workeremployer relationship in the last 10 years?, How has the UK Restaurant sector been affected by the fissuring of the workeremployer relationship in the last 10 years? (2019). london: HMSO.

Patterson, T. E. (2002). The Vanishing Voter: Why Are the Voting Booths So Empty? *National Civic Review*, *91*(4), 367–377. doi: 10.1002/ncr.91407

Pattie, C. J., Seyd, P., & Whiteley, P. (2004). *Citizenship in Britain: values, participation and democracy*. Cambridge: Cambridge University Press.

Pearce, E. (2004). *Reform!: the fight for the 1832 Reform Act*. London: Pimlico.

Pearce, S., & Fox, S. (2016, September 2). Survey evidence: The EU referendum had a clear positive impact on young people's political engagement. Retrieved March 8, 2020, from https://blogs.lse.ac.uk/europpblog/2016/08/26/survey-evidence-the-eu-referendum-had-a-clear-positive-impact-on-young-peoples-political-engagement/

Peterson, D. K. (2013). Slave Rebellions. *The Wiley-Blackwell Encyclopedia of Social and Political Movements*. doi: 10.1002/9780470674871.wbespm486

Petrov, Y. (2014). *Political Participation of Young People How do young people perceive their political participation and their opportunities for participation?* (dissertation). University of gothernberg, Gothernberg.

Pich, C., Harvey, J., Armannsdottir, G., Poorrezaei, M., Branco-Illodo, I., & Kincaid, A. (2018). Marketing Brexit: An exploratory study of young voter engagement in relation to the EU referendum. *International Journal of Market Research, 60*(6), 589–610. doi: 10.1177/1470785318793260

Platts-Fowler, D. (2016). *Beyond the riots: policing in partnership to prevent and contain urban unrest* (dissertation). university of Leeds, Leeds, Leeds.

Prescott, C. (2019, May 23). Internet users, UK: 2019. Retrieved April 6, 2020, from https://www.ons.gov.uk/businessindustryandtrade/itandinternetindustry/bulletins/internetusers/2019

Putnam, R. D. (1995). Bowling Alone: Americas Declining Social Capital. *Journal of Democracy, 6*(1), 65–78. doi: 10.1353/jod.1995.0002

Putnam, R. D. (1995). Tuning In, Tuning Out: The Strange Disappearance of Social Capital in America. *PS: Political Science and Politics*, *28*(4), 664. doi: 10.2307/420517

Rath, K. (2012, August 17). E-petitions get 6.4 million signatures in a year. Retrieved March 19, 2020, from https://www.bbc.co.uk/news/uk-politics-19266497

Reichert, F. (2016). How internal political efficacy translates political knowledge into political participation: Evidence from Germany. *Europe's Journal of Psychology*, *12*(2), 221–241. doi: 10.5964/ejop.v12i2.1095

Rosenstone, S. J., & Hansen, J. M. (2003). *Mobilization, participation, and democracy in America*. New York, NY: Longman.

Rosenstone, S. J., & hansen, john. (2009). *Mobilization, participation, and democracy in america*. Place of publication not identified: Longman.

Shumway, E. S. (1901). Freedom and Slavery in Roman Law. *The American Law Register (1898-1907)*, *49*(11), 636. doi: 10.2307/3306244

Sigel, R. S., Barnes, S. H., & Kaase, M. (1980). Political Action: Mass Participation in Five Western Democracies. *Political Science Quarterly*, *95*(3), 539. doi: 10.2307/2150095

Simpson, I., & Curtice, J. . (2018). *Why Turnout Increased in the 2017 General Election And The Increase Did Not Help Labour*. London: NatCen Social Research.

Sloam, J. (2007). Rebooting Democracy: Youth Participation in Politics in the UK. *Parliamentary Affairs*, *60*(4), 548–567. doi: 10.1093/pa/gsm035

Sloam, J. (2011). 'Rejuvenating Politics? Youth, Citizenship and Politics in the United States and Europe.' *SSRN Electronic Journal*. doi: 10.2139/ssrn.1910527

Sloam, J., & Henn, M. (2018). Youthquake: Young People and the 2017 General Election. *Youthquake 2017*, 91–115. doi: 10.1007/978-3-319-97469-9_5

Sloam, J., Ehsan, R., & Henn, M. (2018). 'Youthquake': How and Why Young People Reshaped the Political Landscape in 2017. *Political Insight*, 9(1), 4–8. doi: 10.1177/2041905818764697

Sloam, J. (2018). #Votebecause: Youth mobilisation for the referendum on British membership of the European Union. *New Media & Society*, 20(11), 4017–4034. doi: 10.1177/1461444818766701

Smith, N., Lister, R., Middleton, S., & Cox, L. (2005). Young People as Real Citizens: Towards an Inclusionary Understanding of Citizenship. *Journal of Youth Studies*, 8(4), 425–443. doi: 10.1080/13676260500431743

Smith, R., Spain, E., & Glancey, R. (2015). Fixed-term Parliaments Act 2011 (2011, c. 14). *Core Statutes on Public Law & Civil Liberties*, 229–230. doi: 10.1007/978-1-137-54504-6_50

Stoker, G. (2006). *Why politics matters: making democracy work.* Basingstoke: Palgrave Macmillan.

Stoker, G. (2017). *Why politics matters: making democracy work.* London: Palgrave.

Stolle, D., Hooghe, M., & Micheletti, M. (2005). Politics in the Supermarket: Political Consumerism as a Form of Political Participation. *International Political Science Review, 26*(3), 245–269. doi: 10.1177/0192512105053784

Stratmann, T., & Okolski, G. (2010). *Civic Participation and Government Spending.* Fairfax, Virginia: t George Mason University.

Students have not forgiven the Liberal Democrats for raising tuition fees. (2017, May 4). Retrieved March 17, 2020, from https://www.economist.com/speakers-corner/2017/05/04/students-have-not-forgiven-the-liberal-democrats-for-raising-tuition-fees

Sturgis, P., & Jennings, W. (2020). Was there a 'Youthquake' in the 2017 general election? *Electoral Studies, 64.*

Teixeira, R. A. (1992). *The disappearing American voter*. Washington, D.C.: Brookings Institution.

The Electoral Commission. (2002). *Voter engagement and young people*. London: The electoral commision.

The Representation of the People (England and Wales) (Description of Electoral Registers and Amendment) Regulations 2013. (n.d.). Retrieved May 18, 2020, from http://www.legislation.gov.uk/en/uksi/2013/3198/schedule/3/chapter/2/made

Tonge, J. (2017). Supplying Confidence or Trouble? The Deal Between the Democratic Unionist Party and the Conservative Party. *The Political Quarterly, 88*(3), 412–416. doi: 10.1111/1467-923x.12411

Treadwell, J., Briggs, D., Winlow, S., & Hall, S. (2012). Shopocalypse Now: Consumer Culture and the English Riots of 2011. *British Journal of Criminology, 53*(1), 1–17. doi: 10.1093/bjc/azs054

Uberoi, E. (2019). *Turnout at elections* . London: Parliament , house of commons.

Umbers, L. M. (2018). Compulsory Voting: A Defence. *British Journal of Political Science*, 1–18. doi: 10.1017/s0007123418000303

van Deth. (2001). Studying Political Participation: Towards a Theory of Everything? *Joint Sessions of Workshops of the European Consortium for Political Research.*

Volacu, A. (2019). Democracy and Compulsory Voting. *Political Research Quarterly*, 106591291983915. doi: 10.1177/1065912919839155

Warren, I. (2017, October 12). How the Conservatives lost their home counties heartland | Ian Warren. Retrieved February 3, 2020, from https://www.theguardian.com/commentisfree/2017/oct/12/conservatives-lost-home-counties-influx-young-people-london-south-east

Wheeler, P. (2015, February 5). Britain's missing voters: why individual registration has been a disaster. Retrieved April 13, 2020, from https://www.theguardian.com/public-leaders-network/2015/feb/05/missing-voters-individual-electoral-registration-disaster

White, I., & Durkin, M. (2007, May 13). General Election Dates 1832-2005. Retrieved May 17, 2020, from https://commonslibrary.parliament.uk/research-briefings/sn04512/

Whiteley, P., Poletti, M., Webb, P., & Bale, T. (2018). Oh Jeremy Corbyn! Why did Labour Party membership soar after the 2015 general election? *The British Journal of Politics and International Relations, 21*(1), 80–98. doi: 10.1177/1369148118815408

Wintour, P. (2015, January 16). 1m voters lost from electoral roll, says Ed Miliband. Retrieved March 18, 2020, from http://www.theguardian.com/politics/2015/jan/16/ed-miliband-1m-voters-fallen-off-electoral-roll

Wolfson, S. (2017, May 18). How do you solve Britain's youth voting crisis? Retrieved May 1, 2020, from https://www.theguardian.com/politics/2017/may/18/how-solve-youth-voting-crisis-voter-registration-election

Wood, A. J. (2020). Beyond mobilisation at McDonald's: Towards networked organising. *Capital & Class*, 030981682090635. doi: 10.1177/0309816820906354

Wright, S. (2012). Assessing (e-)Democratic Innovations: "Democratic Goods" and Downing Street E-Petitions. *Journal of Information Technology & Politics*, 9(4), 453–470. doi: 10.1080/19331681.2012.712820

Younge, G. (2011, August 14). These riots were political. They were looting, not shoplifting | Gary Younge. Retrieved May 16, 2020, from https://www.theguardian.com/commentisfree/2011/aug/14/young-british-rioters-political-actions

Youth membership of unions grows amidst decades of decline. (2020, January 27). Retrieved February 3, 2020, from https://neweconomics.org/2019/05/next-generation-of-union-members-drops-by-half-in-10-years

Zagoria, T., Schulkind, R., & Zagoria, T. (2017, July 18). How Labour activists are already building a digital strategy to win the next election. Retrieved February 2, 2020, from https://www.newstatesman.com/politics/elections/2017/07/how-labour-activists-are-already-building-digital-strategy-win-next

Zukin, C., Keeter, S., & Andolina, M. (2006). *A new engagement? Political participation, civic life, and the changing American citizen.* New York, NY: Oxford University Press.

Printed in Great Britain
by Amazon